101 Martinis

Special thanks to Michael C. Fina for the following glasses loaned to John Wiley & Sons for the photography: Apple Martini (page 23), "Desire" by Hoya; Lychee Martini (page 75), "Springtime Clear" by Varga; Peach Granita Martini (page 82), "Diabolo" by Saint Louis Crystal; Burnt Orange Martini (page 99), "Park Place" by Kate Spade; Tiramisu Martini (page 114), "Dot Collection" by John Hardy; and Chocolate Mint Martini (tall glass in back, page 121), "Vino Grande" by Spiegelau. Michael C. Fina, 545 Fifth Avenue, New York, NY 10017, 1-800-BUY FINA, www.michaelcfina.com

Thanks also to Janet Torelli Handcrafted Sterling Silver, www.martinipic.com, for the ginkgo leaf skewer in the Mai Taini (page 53).

This book is printed on acid-free paper.

Published by John Wiley & Sons, Inc., Hoboken, New Jersey
Published simultaneously in Canada

Book design by Elizabeth Van Itallie
Food styling by Jee Levin
Prop styling by Leslie Siegel

Library of Congress Cataloging-in-Publication Data

Haasarud, Kim.
101 martinis / Kim Haasarud ; photography by Alexandra Grablewski.
p. cm.
Includes index.
ISBN-13 978-0-7645-9985-9 (cloth)
ISBN-10 0-7645-9985-2 (cloth)
1. Martinis. I. Title: One hundred and one martinis. II. Title: One hundred one martinis. III. Title.

TX951.H21 2006
641.8'74--dc22
2005025152

Printed in China

10 9 8 7 6 5 4 3 2 1

KIM HAASARUD

PHOTOGRAPHY BY ALFXANDRA GRABLEWSKI

JOHN WILEY & SONS, INC.

The Evolution *of the* Martini

Some years ago if you walked into a bar and asked for an apple martini, the bartender likely would have met you with a blank stare and said, "Sure . . . what's in that?" Now it's impossible to visit a bar, restaurant, or club without seeing one. The martini we once knew as "gin stirred over ice with a touch of vermouth" is long gone. In its place is a new, sophisticated cocktail with enough variations to please any palate. The martini has evolved into a liquid canvas, for creations both beautiful and delectable. And apart from the traditional gin and vermouth, nearly any ingredient can be used. And I do mean anything: rum, scotch, fruit infusions, ice cream, and even herbal supplements are just a few of the ingredients used in the new wave of nouveau martinis.

The demand for this new wave of martinis has exploded, creating a whole new cocktail culture. People have become savvier drinkers with more sophisticated palates, and what was once "I'll have a Cape Cod" is now "I'll have a Grey Goose Citrus with white cranberry juice straight up with a splash of lime." Even the bartender has been transformed, into the "bar chef."

And it's not just women drinking these martinis. The Cosmopolitan is a perfect example. Once seen almost exclusively as a "chick" drink, the Cosmo has become hip for both sexes. Whether it's happy hour, a bridal shower, a holiday party, or just a friendly gathering, there is a martini to fit the occasion.

How to Make a "Perfect" Martini

The martini craze is not without its dark side. New spirits and mixers are flooding the liquor store shelves as a result of this trend. Some of these are great and some are...well, abominable. (I once came across a forest-green mojito syrup that not only looked dubious, but tasted like liquid toothpaste.) Unfortunately, many martinis are made cheaply, with subpar ingredients. "Fast and easy" doesn't inherently preclude quality. The famous apple martini is a case in point: the typical "mix" looks like neon-green liquid kryptonite and tastes more like a green-apple Jolly Rancher than a real green apple. Try an apple martini made with fresh-pressed apple juice or green apple puree, apple brandy, and high-quality vodka, and you will discover a world of difference. While fresh ingredients may take a little more time to prepare, the results can be spectacular.

So, how does one make the "perfect" martini? Everyone has a foolproof recipe, favorite spirit, or "secret" ingredient, but it's a combination of several factors that makes a "good" martini "perfect":

1. Ingredients. The use of high-quality and fresh ingredients greatly impacts the overall taste of a martini.

2. Balance. Balancing the ingredients is the key to making the martini come together.

3. Time and Place. Brunch? Afternoon wedding reception? Formal cocktail party? After dinner? Holiday? The time and place and even the season make a difference in how one enjoys the cocktail experience. For example, Bellinis and other "light" cocktails (low in alcohol) are most appropriate for brunch while dessert martinis, such as the Ultimate Chocolate Martini and the Bananas Foster Martini, are enjoyable as after-dinner cocktails. Use discretion and pick martinis that are appropriate not only for the occasion, but for the season as well.

4. Personal Taste. This is a top priority. One person may love a dirty gin martini while another may find it absolutely repulsive. Drink what you like, not what others like. There are enough combinations to please any mood or palate, so you can afford to be selective.

PUREES & SYRUPS

Fruit purees are a wonderful addition to a martini. They are fresh, visually appealing, and easy to make. Purees can be made with virtually any fruit. Simply slice or peel (if applicable) a fruit and blend with simple syrup (see following recipe). Typically, 1 to 2 tablespoons of simple syrup to 1 cup of fruit is sufficient. They can also be frozen for later use. Some specialty grocery stores sell premade purees, but you may not find a very big selection. A good selection of purees by Funkin Fruit, a UK-based company, is now available in the U.S. See them at http://www.funkin.us. (Funkin Fruit's "Liquid Chocolate" is to die for! It makes an incredible chocolate martini.) Perfect Puree is another company (based in California) that offers a wide selection of premium purees for cocktails and for cooking. You can find them on the Web at http://www.perfectpuree.com.

Simple SYRUP

Simple syrup is the base used to make most purees. Make some in advance; it can be stored in your refrigerator for weeks.

½ CUP WHITE SUGAR
½ CUP HOT WATER

In a small bowl, glass, or empty clean wine bottle, combine the sugar with the hot water and stir, or shake bottle, until completely dissolved. Let cool completely before using.

Flavored syrups can also be used in lieu of simple syrup. They are convenient and can add flavors that might otherwise be difficult to come by. Monin has a large selection of syrup flavors, including lychee, gingerbread, and lavender, all of which are excellent in cocktails. You may be able to find them at your local grocery store, or go to http://www.monin.com to see their full selecton of flavors.

Martini-Food Pairings

For wine connoisseurs, enjoying the right bottle with the right meal is a much-treasured experience. Now spirit-food pairings are becoming popular as well. With the wide range of ingredients used in cocktails nowadays, they can easily be paired with a variety of foods. Like wine, cocktails and spirits work well with foods that share similar notes and flavors. For example, spicy-savory martinis like the Dirty Bloody Martini and the Inside-Out Bloody Mary can be paired with savory foods such as peppered steak and garlic-stuffed olives. A dessert martini like the White Chocolate Martini pairs nicely with chocolate-covered strawberries or raspberry sorbet. Flavors may also complement one another. For example, the sweetness of the Cantaloupe Martini can be paired with a salty, cured meat like prosciutto. At the end of most of the martinis I have indicated a basic food pairing icon. Please use the icon as a general guide to the types of flavors to pair the martini with, not a hard and fast rule.

WITH SALTY FOOD

Salty Examples: olives, salted nuts, prosciutto, some cheeses, Cuban cuisine

Sweet Examples: pecan pie, crème brûlée, chocolate mousse, ripe tropical fruits

Spicy Examples: Italian sausage, peppered steak, Indian food

Sour Examples: citrus fruit, green apples, lemon sorbet

How to Use this Book

There are several ways to use this book. One is to flip through it and look for something interesting and inspiring that fits the occasion you are planning. Another is to dig through your liquor cabinet and refrigerator and see what spirits and ingredients you already have, and then flip through the book. But my personal recommendation is to take a trip to your local farmer's market or grocery store and see what is fresh and available, and use that as your starting point. Nothing beats a cocktail made with fresh, ripe, seasonal ingredients.

A special note to the martini purists (those who think anything other than straight vodka and/or gin and vermouth is not a martini): My sincerest apologies. Not only did I bend the rules for making a "martini," I bent them back and tied them in a pretty bow. I hope that you at least feel compelled to try a few of these nouveau martinis and judge for yourself. If not, feel free to use this book as a doorstop or fireplace kindling. Cheers!

—Kim Haasarud, The Liquid Chef

Classic
GIN MARTINI

1

The gin martini is the quintessential martini, created in the mid- to late 1800s. It wasn't until a hundred years later that bartenders started using vodka as a regular replacement. For a Classic Vodka Martini, just substitute premium vodka for the gin.

STRIP OF LEMON PEEL (OPTIONAL)
2½ OUNCES PREMIUM GIN
SPLASH OF VERMOUTH (OPTIONAL)
3 SPEARED OLIVES (OPTIONAL)

For a proper lemon twist, rub the lemon peel, yellow side down (not the pith), around the edge of a chilled martini glass. Twist and drop into the glass.

Combine the gin and vermouth in a cocktail shaker filled with ice. Shake and strain into the chilled martini glass. If you didn't use the lemon twist for garnish, then garnish with olives, if desired.

VESPER *(James Bond)* MARTINI

The cocktail described by James Bond in the novel *Casino Royale:* " . . . three measures of Gordon's [gin], one of vodka, and a half-measure of Kina Lillet [aka Lillet Blanc, a type of wine made with fruit, brandy, and herbs—not as bitter as vermouth]. Shake it very well until it's ice cold, then add a large thin slice of lemon peel."

WITH SALTY FOOD

2

3

GIBSON

Both the Gibson and the Gimlet can be served either on the rocks or straight up, depending on preference. For a Vodka Gibson or Gimlet, use vodka in lieu of gin.

2 OUNCES PREMIUM GIN
½ OUNCE DRY VERMOUTH
3 PEARL ONIONS

Combine the gin and vermouth in a cocktail shaker filled with ice. Shake vigorously and strain into a chilled martini glass, or pour over ice in a "rocks" glass. Garnish with the pearl onions.

WITH SALTY FOOD

4

GIMLET

Substitute lime cordial (such as Rose's Lime Juice) for the vermouth and garnish with a lime wedge. Add a splash of soda water, if desired.

WITH SOUR FOOD

5

Very Dirty MARTINI

The traditional dirty martini is made with just a splash of olive juice, but I've found the majority of people who like dirty martinis like them very dirty. If you don't feel like buying a whole jar of olives just for the olive juice, you can buy bottled olive juice from DirtySue.com.

2½ OUNCES PREMIUM GIN OR VODKA
1 OUNCE OLIVE JUICE
3 SPEARED GREEN OLIVES

Combine the vodka and olive juice in a cocktail shaker filled with ice. Shake vigorously and strain into a chilled martini glass. Garnish with the speared olives. (By the way, it's bad luck to serve a martini with less than 3 olives!)

WITH
SALTY
FOOD

6

Dirty Bloody MARTINI

Add a couple of ounces of Bloody Mary mix and a splash of lemon juice for this spicy rendition of the dirty martini. For a spicy dirty martini rim, mix together 1 tablespoon coarse salt with 3 tablespoons Cajun or coarse black pepper. Wet the rim of the martini glass with lemon juice and dip into the salt-pepper mixture.

7

MANHATTAN

2 OUNCES WHISKEY (RYE, BLENDED, OR BOURBON, DEPENDING ON PREFERENCE)
1 OUNCE ITALIAN SWEET VERMOUTH
2 TO 3 DASHES OF ANGOSTURA BITTERS
MARASCHINO CHERRY, FOR GARNISH

Combine the whiskey, vermouth, and bitters in a cocktail shaker filled with ice. Stir and strain into a chilled martini glass. Garnish with maraschino cherry.

WITH SWEET FOOD

Winter MANHATTAN

A variation of the Manhattan using an infused bourbon and apricot brandy.

2 OUNCES CINNAMON-RASPBERRY OR CHERRY-INFUSED BOURBON (SEE NOTE)
1 OUNCE APRICOT BRANDY
2 TO 3 DASHES ANGOSTURA BITTERS
RASPBERRY, OR CHERRY AND CINNAMON STICK, FOR GANISH

8

Combine the infused bourbon, apricot brandy, and bitters in a cocktail shaker filled with ice. Stir and strain into a chilled martini glass. Garnish with a raspberry or a cherry and cinnamon stick.

NOTE: To make cinnamon-raspberry or cherry-infused bourbon, combine 1 bottle of bourbon with 1 pint raspberries or 1½ cups of sliced and pitted cherries and 3 cinnamon sticks, and infuse for 4 to 7 days in a cool, shaded area.

9

Inside Out BLOODY MARY

If you like vodka martinis and Bloody Marys, you'll like this cocktail, too.

3 TO 4 SPICY MARY CUBES (SEE NOTE)
2 OUNCES PEPPER OR LEMON VODKA
SPLASH OF LEMON JUICE
SPLASH OF TABASCO
SMALL CELERY STALK, FOR GARNISH
SPEARED RED CHILE PEPPER, FOR GARNISH (OPTIONAL)

Place the spicy Mary cubes in an empty martini glass. Combine the vodka, lemon juice, and Tabasco in a cocktail shaker filled with ice, shake vigorously, and strain over the Mary cubes. Garnish with a small celery stalk and a chile, if using. The longer you let the martini sit, the more the cubes will infuse into the martini.

NOTE: To make spicy Mary cubes, make your own Bloody Mary mix or buy a premade one and add horseradish, whole olives, or Worcestershire sauce, or whatever else you like to put in your Bloody Mary mix. Pour the spicy Mary mix into ice trays. Place the trays in the freezer and let sit until cubes are frozen.

WITH SALTY FOOD

Cigar MARTINI

Try pairing this with a good cigar.

10

- 1 OUNCE SCOTCH (A BLENDED SCOTCH LIKE JOHNNIE WALKER RED OR BLACK)
- 1 OUNCE TIA MARIA LIQUEUR
- ¾ OUNCE TAWNY PORT

In a mixing glass, combine the scotch, Tia Maria, and port with just a few cubes of ice. Stir lightly, just enough to barely chill the drink, and strain into a martini glass.

WITH SWEET FOOD

Sidecar MARTINI

The traditional sidecar cocktail uses regular brandy. Calvados—distilled apple brandy—gives this classic cocktail a modern edge.

- 1½ OUNCES CALVADOS
- 1 OUNCE COINTREAU
- 1 OUNCE LEMON JUICE
- FOR MARTINI RIM: LEMON JUICE AND SUPERFINE SUGAR ON SEPARATE PLATES

11

Wet the rim of a martini glass with lemon juice. Dip into the superfine sugar and set aside. Combine the Calvados, Cointreau, and 1 ounce lemon juice in a cocktail shaker filled with ice and shake vigorously. Strain into the martini glass.

WITH SOUR FOOD

12 Cosmopolitan

2 ounces red cranberry juice
1 ½ ounces citrus vodka
1 ounce Cointreau
½ ounce lime juice
Orange twist, for garnish

Combine the cranberry juice, vodka, Cointreau, and lime juice in a cocktail shaker filled with ice and shake vigorously. Strain into a chilled martini glass. Garnish with an orange twist.

WITH SOUR FOOD

13 *White* Cosmopolitan

Substitute white cranberry juice for the red cranberry juice for a more refined and elegant Cosmopolitan.

WITH SOUR FOOD

Kiwi COSMO

A lot of variations on the Cosmopolitan can be made using fresh juices and purees. Try experimenting on your own. This is a seasonal cosmopolitan made with kiwis.

1 ½ OUNCES CITRUS VODKA
½ OUNCE COINTREAU
½ OUNCE MIDORI
2 OUNCES WHITE CRANBERRY JUICE
1 ½ OUNCES KIWI PUREE (SEE NOTE)
SPLASH OF LIME JUICE

Combine the vodka, Cointreau, Midori, white cranberry juice, kiwi puree, and lime juice with ice and shake vigorously. Strain into a chilled martini glass.

NOTE: To make kiwi puree, peel 4 kiwis and blend with ½ ounce simple syrup. For a more tropical flavor, you can also add a New Zealand gold kiwi.

14

WITH
SOUR
FOOD

15

Apple MARTINI

2 OUNCES PREMIUM APPLE JUICE OR APPLE CIDER
1 ½ OUNCES CITRUS VODKA
1 OUNCE BERENTZEN'S APPLE LIQUEUR (APPLE BRANDY OR APPLE SCHNAPPS CAN ALSO BE USED)
1 OUNCE GREEN APPLE PUREE (OPTIONAL, FOR A MORE ROBUST MARTINI)
SPLASH OF LEMON JUICE
GREEN APPLE WEDGE, FOR GARNISH

Combine the apple juice, vodka, apple liqueur, apple puree, if using, and lemon juice in a cocktail shaker filled with ice and shake vigorously. Strain into a chilled martini glass. Garnish with an apple wedge.

16

WITH SALTY FOOD

Spiced Apple MARTINI

For a warmer, baked-apple flavor, add a few spices to the traditional Apple Martini just prior to shaking: a few cloves and a dash of cinnamon and nutmeg.

17

Sparkling Apple MARTINI

For a crisper cocktail, substitute sparkling apple cider for the apple juice. Omit the apple puree, and add the sparkling cider last.

Caramel Apple **MARTINI**

MELTED CARAMEL, FOR GARNISH
2½ OUNCES PREMIUM APPLE JUICE OR APPLE CIDER
¾ OUNCE VODKA
¾ OUNCE BERENTZEN'S APPLE LIQUEUR
¾ OUNCE BUTTERSCOTCH SCHNAPPS
GREEN AND/OR RED APPLE SLICE, FOR GARNISH

If making several of these martinis, melt 10 to 15 caramels in a double boiler over low heat, stirring constantly. Once melted, turn off the heat and set aside.

Combine the juice or cider, vodka, apple liqueur, and butterscotch schnapps in a cocktail shaker filled with ice and shake vigorously. Strain into a chilled martini glass. Dip one end of an apple slice (or two) in melted caramel and use it to garnish the edge of the glass.

18

WITH SWEET FOOD

19

Lemon Drop MARTINI

Feel free to add a splash of Cointreau or triple sec to this martini, if desired.

2 OUNCES LEMON OR CITRUS VODKA
1 OUNCE LEMON JUICE
½ OUNCE SIMPLE SYRUP (SEE PAGE 7)
LEMON WHEEL, FOR GARNISH
FOR MARTINI RIM: ¼ CUP SIMPLE SYRUP AND WHITE SUGAR ON SEPARATE PLATES

Wet the rim of a martini glass in simple syrup. Dip into the sugar several times to ensure coverage, and set aside.

Combine the vodka, lemon juice, and simple syrup in a cocktail shaker filled with ice and shake vigorously. Strain into the rimmed martini glass. Garnish with a lemon wheel.

WITH SWEET FOOD

WITH SOUR FOOD

20

Lemon Drop TEQUINI

Substitute 100 percent blue agave tequila for the vodka and increase the simple syrup to 1 ounce for a Mexican version of the Lemon Drop.

WITH SALTY FOOD

21

Blood Orange MARTINI

2½ OUNCES BLOOD ORANGE JUICE
1½ OUNCES GREY GOOSE L'ORANGE VODKA
½ OUNCES GRAND MARNIER
½ OUNCE ORANGE CURAÇAO
½ OUNCE LEMON JUICE
BLOOD ORANGE SLICE, FOR GARNISH

Combine the blood orange juice, vodka, Grand Marnier, orange curaçao, and lemon juice in a cocktail shaker filled with ice and shake vigorously. Strain into a chilled martini glass. Garnish with a blood orange slice.

Grapefruit SQUEEZE

If you can find them, the juice of pomelos (also known as Chinese grapefruits) is excellent in cocktails.

3 OUNCES FRESHLY SQUEEZED GRAPEFRUIT JUICE (ABOUT ½ GRAPEFRUIT)
¾ OUNCE VODKA
¾ OUNCE GIN
½ OUNCE SIMPLE SYRUP (SEE PAGE 7)
1 OUNCE TONIC WATER
GRAPEFRUIT SLICE, FOR GARNISH

Combine the vodka, gin, grapefruit juice, and simple syrup in a cocktail shaker filled with ice and shake moderately. Strain into a chilled martini glass. Top off with tonic water. Garnish with a grapefruit slice.

22

WITH SALTY FOOD

French MARTINI

1 ½ OUNCES PREMIUM VODKA
1 OUNCE FRESH (OR STORE-BOUGHT) PINEAPPLE JUICE
¾ OUNCE CHAMBORD
LEMON PEEL, FOR GARNISH

Combine the vodka, pineapple juice, and Chambord in a cocktail shaker filled with ice and shake vigorously. Strain into a chilled martini glass. Garnish with the lemon peel.

23

WITH SWEET FOOD

Purple Rain MARTINI

24

A variation of the French Martini made with pomegranate-infused sake instead of vodka.

2½ OUNCES POMEGRANATE-INFUSED SAKE (SEE NOTE)
2½ OUNCES PINEAPPLE JUICE
½ OUNCE CHAMBORD

Combine the infused sake, pineapple juice, and Chambord in a cocktail shaker filled with ice and shake vigorously. Strain into a chilled martini glass.

NOTE: To make pomegranate-infused sake, combine 1 liter of sake with the seeds of 2 pomegranates. Let infuse for 1 week. (If pressed for time, combine 2½ ounces sake and ½ ounce pomegranate juice.)

WITH SPICY FOOD

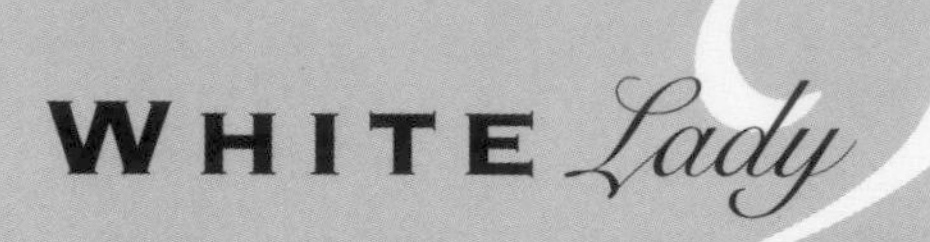

WHITE *Lady*

A classic cocktail from 1920s London.

2 OUNCES GIN
1 OUNCE COINTREAU
1 OUNCE LEMON JUICE
1 EGG WHITE
LEMON SLICE, FOR GARNISH

Combine the gin, Cointreau, lemon juice, and egg white in a cocktail shaker filled with ice and shake vigorously. Strain into a chilled martini glass. Garnish with lemon slice.

PASSIONATE *Lady*

Add ½ ounce passion fruit puree and 1 ounce champagne for a passionate white lady.

Flirtini

Here's the cocktail made famous by the television show *Sex and the City.* There are several versions of this cocktail floating around, but this one is my favorite. It is the creation of master mixologist Dale DeGroff and taken from his *The Craft of the Cocktail.*

2 PIECES OF FRESH PINEAPPLE
½ OUNCE COINTREAU OF TRIPLE SEC
½ OUNCE VODKA
1 OUNCE PINEAPPLE JUICE
3 OUNCES CHAMPAGNE
CHERRY, FOR GARNISH

27

In the bottom of a mixing glass, muddle the pineapple pieces and the Cointreau. Add the vodka and juice and stir with ice. Strain into chilled martini glass and top with the champagne. Garnish with the cherry.

WITH SWEET FOOD

WITH SOUR FOOD

SANGRITINI

1 ORANGE SLICE
1 LEMON SLICE
1 LIME SLICE
½ OUNCE CITRUS OR ORANGE VODKA
½ OUNCE COINTREAU
2½ OUNCES MERLOT WINE (INEXPENSIVE)
1 OUNCE PINEAPPLE JUICE
CHERRY, FOR GARNISH
ORANGE WHEEL, FOR GARNISH

Mash together the fruit slices with the vodka and Cointreau in a cocktail shaker. Add the red wine, pineapple juice, and ice and shake vigorously. Strain into a chilled martini glass. Garnish with a cherry and an orange wheel.

Bellini MARTINI

A great martini for brunches and bridal showers.

1 OUNCE WHITE PEACH PUREE (SEE NOTE)
½ OUNCE VODKA
½ OUNCE PEACH SCHNAPPS
2 TO 3 OUNCES CHAMPAGNE (OR SPARKLING WINE)
SPLASH OF LEMON JUICE
PEACH SLICE, FOR GARNISH

Combine the peach puree, vodka, and peach schnapps in a cocktail shaker filled with ice and shake moderately. Add the champagne and stir gently—do not shake. Strain into a chilled martini glass.

NOTE: To make fresh white peach puree, blend together the flesh of 2 ripe, peeled peaches with about ¾ ounce simple syrup (see page 7). You may want to add more simple syrup if the peaches are not very ripe or if you prefer a sweeter martini.

29

30

White Peach MARTINI

2 OUNCES VODKA
1½ OUNCES PEACH PUREE (SEE NOTE, PAGE 38)
1 OUNCE PEACH SCHNAPPS
SPLASH OF LEMON JUICE

Combine the vodka, peach puree, peach schnapps, and lemon juice in a cocktail shaker filled with ice and shake moderately. Strain into a chilled martini glass.

Peaches-n-Cream MARTINI

A variation of the peach martini made with vanilla vodka and light cream.

1½ OUNCES VANILLA VODKA
1 OUNCE PEACH SCHNAPPS
1 OUNCE PEACH PUREE (SEE NOTE, PAGE 38)
1 OUNCE LIGHT CREAM

Combine the vodka, peach schnapps, peach puree, and light cream in a cocktail shaker filled with ice and shake moderately. Strain into a chilled martini glass.

31

WITH SWEET FOOD

Passion Fruit MARTINI

32

2 OUNCES ORANGE VODKA
1 ½ OUNCES WHITE CRANBERRY JUICE
1 OUNCE COINTREAU
1 OUNCE PASSION FRUIT PUREE
LEMON WEDGE, FOR GARNISH

Combine the vodka, white cranberry juice, Cointreau, and passion fruit puree in a cocktail shaker filled ice and shake vigorously. Strain into a chilled martini glass. Garnish with a lemon wedge.

PINEAPPLE *Champagne* MARTINI

3 OUNCES PINEAPPLE JUICE (FRESH OR STORE-BOUGHT)
1 OUNCE VODKA
3 OUNCES CHAMPAGNE (OR SPARKLING WINE)
PINEAPPLE WEDGE, FOR GARNISH

Combine the pineapple juice and vodka in a cocktail shaker filled with ice and shake vigorously. Add the champagne and stir—do not shake. Strain into a martini glass. Garnish with a pineapple wedge.

33

34

Strawberry MARTINI

- 1½ OUNCES VODKA OR GIN
- 1½ OUNCES STRAWBERRY JUICE (FROM A JUICER)
- 1 OUNCE ORANGE JUICE, FRESHLY SQUEEZED
- ¾ OUNCE SIMPLE SYRUP (SEE PAGE 7)
- ½ OUNCE COINTREAU
- SPLASH OF LEMON JUICE
- STRAWBERRY, FOR GARNISH

Combine the vodka, strawberry juice, orange juice, simple syrup, Cointreau, and lemon juice in a cocktail shaker filled with ice and shake vigorously. Strain into a martini glass. Garnish with a strawberry.

WITH SWEET FOOD

35

Strawberry-Thyme MARTINI

A variation of the Strawberry Martini made with muddled strawberries, thyme, and gin.

- 2 STRAWBERRIES
- 3 SPRIGS THYME, 1 FOR GARNISH
- ¾ OUNCE SIMPLE SYRUP (SEE PAGE 7)
- ½ OUNCE LEMON JUICE
- 2 OUNCES PLYMOUTH GIN
- ½ OUNCE COINTREAU

In a cocktail shaker, mash together the strawberries and 2 sprigs of the thyme with the simple syrup and lemon juice. Add the gin and Cointreau, fill with ice, and shake vigorously. Strain into a chilled martini glass and garnish with the remaining sprig of thyme.

Razzle-Dazzle MARTINI

1 OUNCE RASPBERRY PUREE (SEE NOTE)
2 OUNCES RASPBERRY VODKA
2 OUNCES WHITE CRANBERRY JUICE
SPLASH OF LEMON JUICE
1 RASPBERRY, FOR GARNISH

Pour the raspberry puree into an empty martini glass. Separately, combine the raspberry vodka, white cranberry juice, and lemon juice in a cocktail shaker filled with ice and shake vigorously. Strain over the raspberry puree. Drop in a whole raspberry for garnish.

NOTE: To make your own raspberry puree, blend a pint of fresh raspberries with ½ to 1 ounce simple syrup (see page 7).

WITH SWEET FOOD

36

37

Mango TINI

- 1 ½ OUNCES VODKA
- 1 ½ OUNCES FRESH ORANGE JUICE
- ¾ OUNCE FRUJA MANGO LIQUEUR
- 1 OUNCE MANGO PUREE
- SPLASH OF LEMON JUICE
- MINT SPRIG, FOR GARNISH

Combine the vodka, orange juice, mango liqueur, mango puree, and lemon juice in a cocktail shaker filled with ice. Shake vigorously and strain into a chilled martini glass. Garnish with a mint sprig.

38

Frozen Mango-Mint MARTINI

For a fresh, frozen mango martini, combine the same ingredients in a blender, add a few mint leaves for extra fragrance and color, and blend together with ½ cup of ice. Pour into a martini glass and garnish with a few mint leaves.

Mojito MARTINI

½ LIME, CUT INTO WEDGES
5 TO 7 MINT LEAVES
¾ OUNCE SIMPLE SYRUP (SEE PAGE 7)
2 OUNCES BACARDI LIMON RUM
1 OUNCE SODA WATER
MINT SPRIG, FOR GARNISH

In a mixing glass, mash together the lime wedges, mint leaves, and simple syrup until the mint leaves are fairly crushed and most of the lime juice has been extracted from the lime. Add ice and the Bacardi Limon. Shake vigorously and strain loosely into a martini glass. Top off with soda water. Garnish with a mint sprig.

39

MARGATINI

40

1 ½ OUNCES TEQUILA
1 OUNCE SIMPLE SYRUP (SEE PAGE 7)
¾ OUNCE COINTREAU
½ OUNCE CITRUS VODKA
½ OUNCE LEMON JUICE
½ OUNCE LIME JUICE
LIME WEDGE, FOR GARNISH
FOR MARTINI RIM: ¼ CUP SIMPLE SYRUP AND COARSE SALT ON SEPARATE PLATES

For an optional salt rim, wet the rim of a martini glass with simple syrup and dip into coarse salt. Set aside.

Combine tequila, simple syrup, Cointreau, vodka, lemon juice, and lime juice in a cocktail shaker and shake vigorously. Strain into a martini glass. Garnish with a lime wedge.

WITH SALTY FOOD

Copacocobanana MARTINI

- 1 OUNCE BANANA NECTAR
- ¾ OUNCE BACARDI WHITE RUM
- ¾ BACARDI CÓCO (COCONUT RUM)
- ¾ OUNCE CRÈME DE BANANA
- ½ OUNCE UNSWEETENED COCONUT MILK
- SPLASH AÑEJO RUM (DARK RUM)
- BABY BANANA, FOR GARNISH

Combine the banana nectar, white rum, coconut rum, crème de banana, coconut milk, and dark rum in a cocktail shaker filled with ice and shake vigorously. Strain into a chilled martini glass. Garnish with a baby banana.

41

WITH SWEET FOOD

MAI TAINI

This is an easy, tri-layered martini version of the classic cocktail created by Trader Vic.

- 1 OUNCE WHITE RUM
- 1 OUNCE PINEAPPLE JUICE
- ¾ OUNCE ORANGE CURAÇAO
- ½ OUNCE LIME JUICE
- ½ OUNCE ORGEAT SYRUP (ALMOND SYRUP)
- ½ OUNCE GRENADINE
- ½ OUNCE MYERS RUM (DARK RUM)
- PINEAPPLE CHUNK, FOR GARNISH

Combine the white rum, pineapple juice, orange curaçao, lime juice, and orgeat syrup in a cocktail shaker filled with ice and shake vigorously. Strain into a chilled martini glass. Add the grenadine to the martini—it should sink toward the bottom. Slowly pour in the dark rum along the side of the martini glass—it should layer on the top. Garnish with a skewered chunk of pineapple.

42

WITH SOUR FOOD

43

Blue HAWAIIAN

- 1½ OUNCES COCONUT RUM
- 2½ OUNCES PINEAPPLE JUICE
- 1 OUNCE BLUE CURAÇAO
- PINEAPPLE WEDGE, FOR GARNISH

Combine coconut rum, pineapple juice, and blue curaçao in a cocktail shaker filled with ice and shake vigorously. Strain into a chilled martini glass. Garnish with a pineapple wedge.

WITH SWEET FOOD

44

Green Parrot MARTINI

This is a fun martini to serve at parties. The watermelon slice looks like the tail of a parrot.

- 1 HEAPING TABLESPOON CHOPPED FRESH PINEAPPLE
- 1 OUNCE KIWI PUREE
- 1½ OUNCES VODKA
- 1½ OUNCES FRESH (OR STORE-BOUGHT) PINEAPPLE JUICE
- ½ OUNCE MIDORI (MELON LIQUEUR)
- 1 WEDGE WATERMELON, FOR GARNISH (THE PARROT'S TAIL)

In a cocktail shaker, mash the pineapple together with the kiwi puree. Add ice, the vodka, pineapple juice, and Midori and shake vigorously. Strain into a chilled martini glass. Garnish with a watermelon wedge.

WITH SWEET FOOD

WITH SOUR FOOD

Caribbean MARTINI

2½ OUNCES PINEAPPLE JUICE
1 OUNCE COCONUT RUM
1 OUNCE VANILLA VODKA
½ OUNCE GRENADINE
ORANGE WEDGE, FOR GARNISH

Combine the pineapple juice, coconut rum, vanilla vodka, and grenadine in a cocktail shaker filled with ice and shake vigorously. Strain into a chilled martini glass. Garnish with an orange wedge.

Watermelon MARTINI

Nothing beats a watermelon martini on a summer day! This is a pretty versatile martini, meaning you can use almost any of the white spirits (e.g., gin, vodka, tequila, rum). Bacardi Limon adds just the right amount of lemon and sweetness to complement the watermelon nicely. Feel free to add watermelon schnapps if you prefer a more sour, robust martini. Personally, I like a more subtle, fresh one.

4 OUNCES WATERMELON PUREE (SEE NOTE), OR JUICE
1½ OUNCES BACARDI LIMON RUM
½ OUNCE WATERMELON SCHNAPPS (OPTIONAL)
SPLASH OF LEMON JUICE
BASIL SPRIG AND WATERMELON WEDGE, FOR GARNISH

Combine watermelon puree, Bacardi Limon, and lemon juice in a cocktail shaker filled with ice and shake vigorously. Strain into a chilled martini glass. Garnish with a sprig of basil and a watermelon wedge.

NOTE: To make watermelon puree, chop the watermelon into 1-inch pieces, de-seed, and blend. One medium-sized watermelon makes about 4 cups of puree.

46

WITH SWEET FOOD

Cantaloupe MARTINI

47

3 OUNCES FRESH CANTALOUPE JUICE (FROM A JUICER—
1 CANTALOUPE MAKES ENOUGH FOR 4 TO 5 MARTINIS)
1 ½ OUNCES VODKA
½ OUNCE MIDORI
½ OUNCE SIMPLE SYRUP (SEE PAGE 7)
SPLASH OF LEMON JUICE
MELON BALLS, FOR GARNISH

Combine cantaloupe juice, vodka, Midori, simple syrup, and lemon juice in a cocktail shaker filled with ice and shake vigorously. Strain into a chilled martini glass. Garnish with melon balls on a skewer.

WITH SALTY FOOD

Honeydew MARTINI

48

Similar to the Cantaloupe Martini, but not as sweet.

- 4 OUNCES FRESH HONEYDEW JUICE (MADE IN A JUICER—1 HONEYDEW MAKES ENOUGH FOR ABOUT 4 MARTINIS)
- 2 OUNCES CITRUS VODKA
- ½ OUNCE MIDORI
- SPLASH OF LIME JUICE
- HONEYDEW SLICE OR MELON BALL, FOR GARNISH

Combine honeydew juice, vodka, Midori, and lime juice in a cocktail shaker filled with ice and shake vigorously. Strain into a chilled martini glass. Garnish with a slice or ball of honeydew.

Sake MARTINI

49

- 3 VERY THIN CUCUMBER SLICES
- 1½ OUNCES VODKA
- 1½ OUNCES SAKE
- 1 OUNCE PLUM WINE

Place the cucumber slices in an empty martini glass. Combine the vodka, sake, and plum wine in a cocktail shaker filled with ice and shake vigorously. Strain over the cucumber slices in the martini glass.

WITH SALTY FOOD

Roasted Ginger MARTINI

This was created by my friend Radha Mehta, a fabulous film production designer in Los Angeles. While making Indian food for friends, she created a ginger infusion cocktail to accompany the spicy Indian cuisine.

50

- **2½ OUNCES GINGER-SAKE OR GINGER-VODKA INFUSION (SEE NOTE)**
- **1 OUNCE SIMPLE SYRUP (SEE PAGE 7)**
- **2 OUNCES FRUIT JUICE OF CHOICE, SUCH AS PASSION FRUIT OR MANGO (OPTIONAL)**
- **MINT LEAVES AND/OR LEMONGRASS, FOR GARNISH**

Combine the ginger infusion and simple syrup in a cocktail shaker filled with ice. Add fruit juice, if desired, and shake vigorously. Strain into a chilled martini glass. Garnish with mint leaves and/or lemongrass.

NOTE: To make a ginger infusion, peel 1 to 2 fingers of fresh ginger and slice into thin strips. Wrap in aluminum foil and roast in a 300°F oven until the ginger starts to sweat, 15 to 20 minutes. Pour a small amount of the vodka or sake out of a liter-sized bottle, add the roasted ginger to the bottle, and let steep in a cool, dark space overnight.

Pineapple Ginger MARTINI

- **2 SLIVERS FRESH GINGER**
- **1 HEAPING TABLESPOON CHOPPED FRESH PINEAPPLE**
- **2 OUNCES VODKA**
- **½ OUNCE LEMON JUICE**
- **½ OUNCE SIMPLE SYRUP** **(SEE PAGE 7)**
- **1 OUNCE GINGER BEER**
- **FRESH SAGE LEAF, FOR GARNISH**

In a cocktail shaker, mash together the fresh ginger and pineapple. Add the vodka, lemon juice, and simple syrup, fill with ice, and shake vigorously. Strain into a chilled martini glass. Top off with ginger beer. Garnish with a fresh sage leaf.

51

WITH
SALTY
FOOD

52

Pearadise MARTINI

1½ OUNCES MATHILDE PEAR LIQUEUR
1½ OUNCES PEAR NECTAR (OR PEAR PUREE)
1 OUNCE HENDRICK'S GIN
SPLASH OF LEMON JUICE
PEAR WEDGE, FOR GARNISH

Combine the pear liqueur, pear nectar, Hendrick's gin, and lemon juice in a cocktail shaker filled with ice and shake vigorously. Strain into a chilled martini glass. Garnish with a pear wedge.

WITH SALTY FOOD

53

Pear-Lavender MARTINI

For a floral flavor, make the recipe above using gin infused with lavender and Asian pears.

To make the infusion, add 2 sliced Asian pears and 15 lavender buds to 1 liter of gin and let sit at least 8 hours or overnight. You can also infuse sake in this way.

Lemongrass MARTINI

54

- **1 TABLESPOON SWEETENED LEMONGRASS (ABOUT ½ STALK, SEE NOTE)**
- **1½ OUNCES VODKA**
- **1 OUNCE SAKE**
- **½ OUNCE LEMON JUICE**

In a cocktail shaker, mash the sweetened lemongrass together with the vodka, sake, and lemon juice. Add ice and shake vigorously. Strain into a chilled martini glass. Garnish with a strip of the lemongrass skin.

NOTE: To prepare the lemongrass, peel away the outer layer of skin from the stalk, exposing the bright, soft yellow layers underneath. Chop and sauté 1 tablespoon of lemongrass with ½ ounce simple syrup (see page 7) about 1 minute, or until soft. This can be used immediately or saved for later.

Lemongrass-Blueberry MARTINI

55

For a fruitier version, add a few blueberries during the mashing process.

Lavender TINI

1 LAVENDER BUD FOR GARNISH
1 ¼ OUNCES VODKA (SEE NOTE)
¾ OUNCE PARFAIT AMOUR LIQUEUR
1 OUNCE LAVENDER SYRUP (MONIN)
2 OUNCES WHITE CRANBERRY JUICE
SPLASH OF LEMON JUICE
LAVENDER SPRIG, FOR GARNISH

In a cocktail shaker, combine the vodka, Parfait Amour liqueur, white cranberry juice, lemon juice, and ice and shake vigorously. Strain into a chilled martini glass. Garnish with a sprig of lavender or float a lavender bud on top.

NOTE: You can also make a lavender-infused vodka to use in lieu of regular vodka. Infuse 15 lavender buds in 1 bottle of vodka for at least 48 hours in a cool, dark place. Strain and bottle.

56

Hibiscus-Rose TEANI

57

This beautiful, deep-pink martini—great for brunches or early afternoons—was created by Radha Mehta. Modern Spirits, an artisanal infused-vodka company based in southern California, makes a rose-petal vodka that is outstanding. If you can find it, use it!

- 3 TO 5 MINT LEAVES
- 1 OUNCE SIMPLE SYRUP (SEE PAGE 7)
- 2 OUNCES VODKA
- 2 OUNCES STEEPED AND CHILLED HIBISCUS TEA
- 3 ROSE PETALS, FOR GARNISH

In a cocktail shaker, mash the mint leaves with the simple syrup. Add the vodka and hibiscus tea, fill with ice, and shake vigorously. Strain into a chilled martini glass. Float rose petals on top, for garnish.

Pomegranate MARTINI

58

1 ½ OUNCES CITRUS OR ORANGE VODKA
1 ½ OUNCES POM WONDERFUL JUICE
1 OUNCE GRAPEFRUIT JUICE
½ OUNCE LEMON JUICE
½ OUNCE SIMPLE SYRUP (SEE PAGE 7)
SPLASH OF COINTREAU
LIME TWIST, FOR GARNISH

Combine the vodka, pomegranate juice, grapefruit juice, lemon juice, simple syrup, and Cointreau in a cocktail shaker filled with ice and shake vigorously. Strain into a chilled martini glass. Garnish with a lime twist.

WITH SWEET FOOD

WITH SOUR FOOD

Elderflower MARTINI

59

- 1½ OUNCES HENDRICK'S GIN
- 1½ OUNCES ELDERFLOWER CORDIAL
- ½ OUNCE DRY VERMOUTH
- SPLASH OF LIME JUICE
- HONEYSUCKLE BLOSSOM OR OTHER SMALL FLOWER, FOR GARNISH

Combine the gin, elderflower cordial, vermouth, and lime juice in a cocktail shaker filled with ice and shake vigorously. Strain into a chilled martini glass. Garnish with a honeysuckle blossom or other small flower.

Lychee MARTINI

60

If you are lucky enough to find them during their short season in the summer, try mashing the flesh of one lychee with the vodka before combining the ingredients.

1 ½ OUNCES VODKA
1 OUNCE LYCHEE SYRUP (MONIN MAKES A GREAT LYCHEE SYRUP)
1 OUNCE LEMON JUICE
½ OUNCE LIGHT RUM
LYCHEE FRUIT, FOR GARNISH

Combine the vodka, lychee syrup, lemon juice, and light rum in a cocktail shaker filled with ice and shake vigorously. Strain into a chilled martini glass. Add a lychee fruit.

Persimmon MARTINI

1 ½ OUNCES VODKA
1 ½ OUNCES CAPTAIN MORGAN'S SPICED RUM
½ OUNCE GRAPEFRUIT JUICE
1 HEAPING TABLESPOON CHOPPED VERY RIPE PERSIMMON FRUIT FLESH
DASH OF CINNAMON AND/OR NUTMEG, FOR GARNISH

61

Combine the vodka, spiced rum, grapefruit juice, and persimmon flesh in a cocktail shaker filled with ice and shake vigorously. Strain into a chilled martini glass. Garnish with a dash of cinnamon and/or nutmeg.

WITH SWEET FOOD

62

Starfruit Blossom MARTINI

2 SLICES STARFRUIT (ABOUT ½ INCH THICK)
½ OUNCE SIMPLE SYRUP **(SEE PAGE 7)**
1 OUNCE LEMON JUICE
2 OUNCES HANGAR ONE MANDARIN BLOSSOM VODKA

In a cocktail shaker, mash 1 starfruit slice together with the simple syrup and lemon juice until entirely pulped. Add the vodka, fill with ice, and shake vigorously. Strain into a chilled martini glass. Garnish with the other starfruit slice, either on the edge of the martini glass or on a skewer.

WITH SWEET FOOD

WITH SOUR FOOD

Lemon Granita MARTINI

63

Perfect for small summer parties.

- ½ OUNCE COINTREAU
- ½ CUP LEMON GRANITA (SEE NOTE)
- 3 OUNCES TROPICAL FRUIT JUICE
- 2 OUNCES ORANGE VODKA

Pour the Cointreau into a martini glass and swirl until the sides have been coated. Add the lemon granita. Add the tropical fruit juice and orange vodka and serve.

NOTE: To make lemon granita, combine equal parts lemon juice and simple syrup (see page 7) and freeze in a baking pan. Once frozen, scrape the ice.

Apricot-Mango MARTINI

2 OUNCES APRICOT NECTAR
1½ OUNCES PLYMOUTH GIN
1 OUNCE APRICOT BRANDY
1 OUNCE MANGO PUREE
SPLASH OF LEMON JUICE
LEMON PEEL, FOR GARNISH

Combine the apricot nectar, gin, apricot brandy, mango puree, and lemon juice in a cocktail shaker filled with ice and shake vigorously. Strain into a chilled martini glass. Garnish with the lemon peel.

WITH SALTY FOOD

WITH SWEET FOOD

64

Peach Granita MARTINI

65

- ½ OUNCE PEACH SCHNAPPS
- ½ CUP PEACH GRANITA (SEE NOTE)
- 3 OUNCES WHITE CRANBERRY-PEACH JUICE
- 1½ OUNCES VODKA (OR ABSOLUT APEACH VODKA)

Pour the peach schnapps in a martini glass and swirl until the sides have been coated. Add the peach granita. Add the juice and vodka.

NOTE: To make peach granita, combine 2 parts peach puree, 2 parts simple syrup (see page 7), and 1 part lemon juice and freeze in a baking pan. Once frozen, scrape the ice.

Blood Cherry MARTINI

66

4 BING CHERRIES, PLUS AN EXTRA FOR GARNISH
½ OUNCE GRAND MARNIER
1 ½ OUNCES VODKA
1 ½ OUNCES BLOOD ORANGE JUICE (THE JUICE OF ONE BLOOD ORANGE)
SPLASH OF MARASCHINO LIQUEUR

In a cocktail shaker, mash the bing cherries together with the Grand Marnier. Add the vodka and blood orange juice and fill with ice. Shake vigorously and set aside. Splash a small amount of the maraschino liqueur into a martini glass. Swirl a few times to completely coat the inside of the martini glass and discard the rest. Strain the drink into the coated martini glass. Drop a bing cherry into the glass for garnish.

67

Rainier (White Cherry) MARTINI

- 2 OUNCES VODKA
- 1 ½ OUNCES RAINIER CHERRY PUREE (SEE NOTE)
- ½ OUNCE LEMON JUICE
- ½ OUNCE SIMPLE SYRUP (SEE PAGE 7)
- 2 TO 3 DASHES OF ANGOSTURA BITTERS
- CHERRY WITH STEM, FOR GARNISH

Combine the vodka, cherry puree, lemon juice, simple syrup, and bitters in a cocktail shaker filled with ice and shake vigorously. Strain into a chilled martini glass. Garnish the rim of the glass with a cherry.

NOTE: To make Rainier cherry puree, in a blender, combine about a dozen pitted Rainier cherries with ½ ounce simple syrup (see page 7). Blend until smooth.

68

Bitter Cherry MARTINI

For a bitter version, replace the Angostura bitters with ¾ ounce Campari.

Plumcot MARTINI

The plumcot, a delicious apricot-plum hybrid, is excellent in cocktails. The flesh is bright purple and firmer than a regular plum, while the skin is tart. Plumcots can be found at most farmers' markets during the summer.

2½ OUNCES PLYMOUTH GIN
1½ OUNCES PLUMCOT PUREE (SEE NOTE)
½ OUNCE LEMON JUICE
½ OUNCE SIMPLE SYRUP (SEE PAGE 7)
MINT LEAF, FOR GARNISH

69

Combine the gin, plumcot puree, lemon juice, and simple syrup in a cocktail shaker filled with ice and shake vigorously. Strain into a chilled martini glass. Garnish with a mint leaf.

NOTE: To make plumcot puree, in a blender, combine 5 plumcots (cored and peeled) with ½ ounce simple syrup (see page 7). Blend until smooth. Makes enough for 4 to 5 martinis.

70

Mistletoe MARTINI

Glögg is a Swedish mulled wine usually served over the holidays, but there are some alcohol-free versions available. I recommend making this cocktail with the alcohol-free version so the kids will have something to drink, too.

1 OUNCE GLÖGG (SOLD AT MANY SPECIALTY GROCERY STORES AND IKEA)
1½ OUNCES ORANGE VODKA
3 OUNCES SPARKLING APPLE CIDER
MISTLETOE, FOR GARNISH

Combine the glögg and vodka in a cocktail shaker filled with ice and shake vigorously. Strain into a chilled martini glass. Top off with sparkling apple cider. Garnish the edge of the martini glass with a small sprig of mistletoe or rosemary sprig, and the cocktail itself with 3 floating cranberries.

Crantopia MARTINI

I created this cocktail on the fly at my in-laws one Thanksgiving. My sister-in-law made this amazing cranberry relish, and I got inspired to create a cocktail with it. You may need to adjust the amount of simple syrup, depending on how sweet or sour the cranberry relish is.

71

- ¾ TABLESPOON CRANBERRY RELISH (NOT CANNED)
- 2 OUNCES RED CRANBERRY JUICE
- 1½ OUNCES ORANGE VODKA
- SIMPLE SYRUP (SEE PAGE 7), TO TASTE
- ROSEMARY SPRIG, FOR GARNISH

Combine the cranberry relish, cranberry juice, orange vodka, and simple syrup to taste in a cocktail shaker filled with ice and shake vigorously. Strain into a chilled martini glass. Garnish with a rosemary sprig.

If the cranberry sauce you are using is fairly thick and chunky, you can combine everything in a blender with a few cubes of ice instead. You can actually quadruple the recipe and make four martinis at once using this method.

Black Currant MARTINI

72

- 4 RED OR BLACK CURRANTS
- 4 BLACK SEEDLESS GRAPES
- 1½ OUNCES ABSOLUT KURANT VODKA
- 1 OUNCE CRANBERRY JUICE
- ½ OUNCE CRÈME DE CASSIS
- SPLASH OF SIMPLE SYRUP (SEE PAGE 7)
- SPEARED CURRANTS AND BLACK GRAPES, FOR GARNISH

In a cocktail shaker, mash together the currants and black grapes until most of the juice has been completely extracted from the fruit. Add the vodka, cranberry juice, crème de cassis, simple syrup, and ice and shake vigorously. Strain into a chilled martini glass. For garnish, spear together a few currants and black grapes, in alternate succession.

Candy Cane MARTINI

73

1½ OUNCES VANILLA VODKA
1½ OUNCES WHITE CRÈME DE CACAO
½ OUNCE PEPPERMINT SCHNAPPS
1 PEPPERMINT CANDY, FOR GARNISH
FOR MARTINI RIM: ½ CUP CRUSHED CANDY CANE (OR PEPPERMINT CANDIES) AND ¼ CUP SIMPLE SYRUP (SEE PAGE 7) ON SEPARATE PLATES

Place the candy cane or peppermint candies on a plate, cover with a napkin, and crush with a heavy object, or crush the candy in a blender; the pieces should only be a tad larger than coarse sand. Dip the rim of a martini glass in simple syrup and then into the peppermint mixture.

Combine the vodka, white crème de cacao, and peppermint schnapps in a cocktail shaker filled with ice and shake vigorously. Strain into the rimmed martini glass. Drop a peppermint candy in the glass.

Pumpkin MARTINI

This is an excellent martini, but the pumpkin liqueur can be difficult to find. You can also make it with pumpkin puree and pumpkin-infused vodka.

1½ OUNCES BOLS PUMPKIN SMASH LIQUEUR
1 OUNCE LIGHT CREAM
¾ OUNCE SPICED RUM
½ OUNCE AMARETTO
TOASTED PUMPKIN SEEDS AND GROUND NUTMEG, FOR GARNISH

Combine the pumpkin liqueur, light cream, spiced rum, and amaretto in a cocktail shaker filled with ice and shake moderately. Strain into a chilled martini glass. Garnish with toasted pumpkin seeds and a dash of nutmeg.

74

WITH SWEET FOOD

Toasted Almond MARTINI

75

1½ OUNCES LIGHT CREAM
¾ OUNCE AMARETTO
¾ OUNCE KAHLUA
½ OUNCE BAILEY'S IRISH CREAM
ALMOND SLIVERS, FOR GARNISH

Toast the almond slivers in a dry skillet over medium heat until they just start to turn golden. Set aside.

Combine the light cream, amaretto, Kahlua, and Bailey's in a cocktail shaker filled with ice and shake moderately. Strain into a chilled martini glass. Sprinkle the martini with the toasted almond slivers.

Burnt Orange MARTINI

1 ORANGE
1 ½ OUNCES WHITE CRÈME DE CACAO
1 OUNCE ORANGE VODKA
½ OUNCE GRAND MARNIER
SPLASH OF LICOR 43

To make burnt orange slices, slice the orange horizontally as thinly as possible. Place the slices on aluminum foil on a sheet pan. Broil for 5 to 8 minutes, or until orange slices start to crisp. Set aside and let cool.

Combine the white crème de cacao, orange vodka, Grand Marnier, and Licor 43 in a cocktail shaker filled with ice. Shake moderately and strain into a chilled martini glass. Float a burnt orange slice on top for garnish.

76

77

Orange Dreamsicle MARTINI

4 OUNCES FRESH ORANGE JUICE
2 OUNCES VANILLA LIQUEUR (E.G., MCGILLICUDDY'S VANILLA SCHNAPPS)
½ OUNCE BACARDI O RUM
ORANGE SLICE, FOR GARNISH
POPSICLE STICK, FOR GARNISH

Combine the orange juice, vanilla liqueur, and Bacardi O in a cocktail shaker filled with ice and shake vigorously. Strain into a chilled martini glass. Garnish with an orange slice and a popsicle stick.

WITH SWEET FOOD

WITH SOUR FOOD

Lemon Meringue MARTINI

78

1½ OUNCES LEMON VODKA
½ OUNCE COINTREAU
1 OUNCE LEMON JUICE
1 OUNCE SIMPLE SYRUP (SEE PAGE 7)
1 LARGE EGG WHITE
POWDERED SUGAR, FOR GARNISH
1 STRIP OF LEMON PEEL, FOR GARNISH

Combine the vodka, Cointreau, lemon juice, simple syrup, and egg white in a cocktail shaker filled with ice and shake extremely well, at least 20 seconds. Strain into the martini glass. Sprinkle with powdered sugar and drop in lemon peel.

Key Lime Pie
MARTINI

1½ ounces Licor 43
1½ ounces key lime juice
1 ounce vanilla vodka
½ ounce Midori
Key lime or a lime wedge, for garnish
For martini rim: key lime juice, simple syrup, (see page 7), and graham cracker crumbs

To coat the rim of a martini glass, pour a small amount of key lime juice and simple syrup in a small plate. In another small plate, pour about 5 tablespoons of graham cracker crumbs. Wet the martini glass rim with the lime juice/simple syrup. Dip into the graham mixture several times to ensure coverage. Set aside.

Combine the Licor 43, key lime juice, vanilla vodka, and Midori in a cocktail shaker filled with ice and shake vigorously. Strain into the rimmed martini glass. Garnish with lime wedge.

79

80

Pink FLAMINGO

Inspired by the classic Pink Squirrel cocktail, this martini uses the South American fruit cherimoya for a more exotic flavor. When a cherimoya is ripe, the fruit will be extremely soft and the skin will start to brown (and will almost break with a light touch.)

- **1 OUNCE LICOR 43**
- **1 OUNCE CRÈME DE NOYAUX**
- **1 OUNCE LIGHT CREAM**
- **1 SPOONFUL RIPE CHERIMOYA FLESH**

Cut the cherimoya fruit lengthwise and scoop out flesh with a spoon. Flesh should be very soft and easy to scoop. Be careful to discard all the seeds, because they are very bitter. Combine the Licor 43, *crème de noyaux*, light cream, and cherimoya in a cocktail shaker filled with ice and shake vigorously. Strain into a chilled martini glass.

Alaskan Ice Cap MARTINI

2 OUNCES VANILLA SOY MILK
1 ½ OUNCES WHITE CRÈME DE CACAO
½ OUNCE PEPPERMINT SCHNAPPS
POWDERED SUGAR, FOR GARNISH
SWEETENED, FINELY SHREDDED COCONUT, FOR MARTINI RIM

Wet the rim of a martini glass with white crème de cacao. Dip into the shredded coconut. If the coconut does not adhere to the martini glass, try chopping it into finer pieces in a blender.

Combine the soy milk, white crème de cacao, and peppermint schnapps in a cocktail shaker filled with ice and shake moderately. Strain into the rimmed martini glass. Sprinkle with powdered sugar.

81

White Chocolate MARTINI

82

1½ OUNCES WHITE CRÈME DE CACAO
1 OUNCE STOLI VANIL VODKA
1 OUNCE LIGHT CREAM (OR HALF-AND-HALF)
½ OUNCE GODIVA WHITE CHOCOLATE LIQUEUR
SPLASH OF LICOR 43
5 OUNCES MELTED WHITE CHOCOLATE, FOR MARTINI RIM
STRAWBERRY, FOR GARNISH (OPTIONAL)

Dip the rim of a martini glass in the melted white chocolate until completely covered. Let cool and set aside. If serving with strawberries, dip them into the melted white chocolate.

Combine white crème de cocoa, vanilla vodka, light cream, Godiva white chocolate liqueur, and Licor 43 in a cocktail shaker filled with ice and shake moderately. Strain into the rimmed martini glass. Garnish with a dipped strawberry, if desired.

Ultimate Chocolate MARTINI

Funkin Fruit is a London-based company that creates freshly made purees (no preservatives) including an amazing "Liquid Chocolate" that is made with Belgian chocolate; I would highly recommend it for the ultimate chocolate martini (www.funkin.us).

- 2 OUNCES GODIVA CHOCOLATE LIQUEUR
- 1 OUNCE VANILLA VODKA
- 1 OUNCE LIGHT CREAM (OR HALF-AND-HALF)
- 1 OUNCE MELTED SEMISWEET CHOCOLATE (OR FUNKIN FRUIT'S "LIQUID CHOCOLATE")
- SWEETENED COCOA POWDER, FOR MARTINI RIM

Wet the rim of a martini glass with Godiva chocolate liqueur. Dip the rim in sweetened cocoa powder several times to ensure complete coverage. Set aside.

Combine the chocolate liqueur, vanilla vodka, light cream, and melted chocolate in a cocktail shaker filled with ice and shake vigorously. Strain into the martini glass.

WITH SWEET FOOD

84

Hot Chocolate MARTINI

- **3 OUNCES HOMEMADE HOT CHOCOLATE, COOLED**
- **1 OUNCE DARK CRÈME DE COCOA**
- **1 OUNCE BAILEY'S IRISH CREAM**
- **¾ OUNCE VANILLA VODKA**
- **3 TO 4 MINIATURE MARSHMELLOWS**

Combine the chocolate, dark crème de cacao, Bailey's, and vanilla vodka in a cocktail shaker filled with ice and shake moderately. Strain into a chilled martini glass. Drop 3 to 4 miniature marshmallows in the glass and roast with a crème brûlée torch, if desired.

Chocolate-Covered Cherry MARTINI

85

- 1 OUNCE GODIVA CHOCOLATE LIQUEUR
- 1 OUNCE VANILLA VODKA
- 1 OUNCE WHITE CRÈME DE CACAO
- ½ OUNCE GRENADINE
- MARASCHINO CHERRY, FOR GARNISH

Combine the Godiva chocolate liqueur, vanilla vodka, white crème de cacao, and grenadine in a cocktail shaker filled with ice and shake vigorously. Strain into a chilled martini glass. Garnish with a cherry.

WITH SWEET FOOD

Cappuccino MARTINI

- 2 OUNCES CHILLED ESPRESSO
- 1½ OUNCES VANILLA VODKA
- 1 OUNCE NOCELLO (WALNUT LIQUEUR)
- 1 OUNCE LIGHT CREAM
- 3 ESPRESSO BEANS, FOR GARNISH

Combine the chilled espresso, vanilla vodka, Nocello, and light cream in a cocktail shaker filled with ice and shake vigorously. Strain into a chilled martini glass. Float 3 espresso beans on top.

86

WITH SWEET FOOD

87

Espresso MARTINI

3 OUNCES CHILLED ESPRESSO
1½ OUNCES PREMIUM VODKA
½ OUNCE KAHLÚA
3 ESPRESSO BEANS, FOR GARNISH

Combine the chilled espresso, vodka, and Kahlúa in a cocktail shaker filled with ice and shake moderately. Strain into a chilled martini glass. Float 3 espresso beans on top.

WITH SWEET FOOD

88

Italian Roast Espresso MARTINI

Add a splash of Sambuca for an Italian espresso martini.

WITH SWEET FOOD

Tiramisu MARTINI

This martini requires a little more skill to perfect the layering technique. Makes a great dessert! Dip the biscotti into the martini, and eat and drink at the same time.

1 OUNCE KAHLÚA
1½ OUNCES CHILLED ESPRESSO
½ OUNCE STOLI VANIL VODKA
½ OUNCE WHITE CRÈME DE CACAO
1 OUNCE LIGHT CREAM
½ OUNCE SIMPLE SYRUP (SEE PAGE 7)
1 LARGE EGG WHITE (OPTIONAL)
CHOCOLATE SHAVINGS, FOR GARNISH

First, combine the Kahlúa and chilled espresso directly in the martini glass. Next, combine the vanilla vodka, white crème de cacao, light cream, simple syrup, and egg white (optional) in a cocktail shaker filled with ice and shake vigorously. Strain carefully into the martini glass so that it layers on top of the espresso layer. You may tip the martini glass slightly to pour down the sides or pour over a spoon so that it layers more easily. Sprinkle with chocolate shavings.

WITH SWEET FOOD

89

Chai TEANI

90

Great for brunches and high tea.

- 2 OUNCES APPLE JUICE
- 1½ OUNCES CHAI-INFUSED VODKA (SEE NOTE)
- ½ OUNCE B & B LIQUEUR
- RED APPLE SLICE, FOR GARNISH (THE SPECKLED SKIN OF GALA APPLES LOOKS GREAT)

Combine the apple juice, chai-infused vodka, and B & B liqueur in a cocktail shaker filled with ice and shake vigorously. Strain into a chilled martini glass. Garnish with a new chai tea bag and/or red apple slice.

NOTE: To make chai-infused vodka, add 1 chai tea bag to 4 ounces of vodka and let infuse for at least 20 minutes.

WITH SWEET FOOD

Oatmeal Cookie MARTINI

- 3/4 ounce Bailey's Irish Cream
- 3/4 ounce butterscotch schnapps
- 1/2 ounce Goldschläger
- 1/2 ounce Jägermeister (optional)
- Splash of light cream
- 3 to 5 raisins, for garnish
- For martini rim: simple syrup (see page 7), and cinnamon sugar, on separate plates

Wet the rim of a martini glass with simple syrup and dip into cinnamon sugar several times to ensure coverage. Set martini glass aside.

Combine Bailey's Irish Cream, Goldschläger, butterscotch schnapps, Jägermeister (if desired), and light cream in a cocktail shaker filled with ice. Shake moderately and strain into the cinnamon sugar–rimmed martini glass. Garnish with 3 to 5 skewered raisins.

91

Bananas Foster MARTINI

92

2 OUNCES DARK AGED RUM
3 TO 4 DASHES OF ANGOSTURA BITTERS
1¾ OUNCES BANANA NECTAR
½ OUNCE CRÈME DE BANANA

Combine ½ ounce of the rum and the bitters in a martini glass. Swirl and carefully light the mixture in the martini glass with a lighter. (It may take a few flicks of the lighter to get it to light, but the key is in the swirling.) Keep swirling until the mixture starts to caramelize (change color) and coats the side of the glass. Discard the remaining liquid and set the martini glass aside.

Combine the remaining 1½ ounces rum, banana nectar, and crème de banana in a cocktail shaker filled with ice and shake vigorously. Strain into the coated martini glass.

Moroccan Mint TEANI

A subtle, light mint martini. Great for a brunch or high tea.

3 OUNCES VANILLA SOY MILK
1½ OUNCES MOROCCAN MINT-INFUSED VODKA (SEE NOTE)
½ OUNCE VANILLA SCHNAPPS (E.G., MCGILLICUDDY'S)
½ OUNCE SIMPLE SYRUP (SEE PAGE 7)
MINT LEAF, FOR GARNISH

Combine the soy milk, Moroccan mint–infused vodka, vanilla schnapps, and simple syrup in a cocktail shaker filled with ice and shake vigorously. Strain into a chilled martini glass. Float a mint leaf on top.

NOTE: To prepare Moroccan mint–infused vodka, steep one Moroccan mint tea bag in 5 ounces vodka for at least 20 minutes. This will be enough for 3 martinis. If you are unable to find Moroccan mint, use equal parts mint and green tea.

93

Chocolate Mint MARTINI

A great after-dinner martini.

1 ½ OUNCES WHITE CRÈME DE COCOA
1 OUNCE VANILLA VODKA
1 OUNCE LIGHT CREAM (OR HALF-AND-HALF)
½ OUNCE GREEN CRÈME DE MENTHE
CHOCOLATE STICK, FOR GARNISH
CHOCOLATE SHAVINGS OR SWEETENED CHOCOLATE POWDER, FOR MARTINI RIM

For a chocolate rim, wet the martini glass rim with white crème de cacao. Dip into sweetened cocoa powder or chocolate shavings several times to ensure coverage. Set aside.

Combine the white crème de cacao, vodka, light cream, and green crème de menthe in a cocktail shaker filled with ice and shake moderately. Strain into the rimmed martini glass. Garnish with a chocolate stick.

94

WITH SWEET FOOD

95

Limon TEANI

2 OUNCES FRESH-BREWED TEA, CHILLED (E.G., LIPTON)
1½ OUNCES BACARDI LIMON RUM
½ OUNCE LEMON JUICE
½ OUNCE SIMPLE SYRUP (SEE PAGE 7)
TEA BAG, FOR ADDED FLAVOR
LEMON WEDGE, FOR GARNISH

Combine the brewed tea, Bacardi Limon, lemon juice, and simple syrup in a cocktail shaker filled with ice and shake vigorously. Strain into a chilled martini glass. Serve with a new tea bag in the martini for added tea flavor. Garnish with a lemon wedge.

96

Green TEANI

Use chilled green tea and vanilla vodka for this light, green tea martini.

2 OUNCES CHILLED, STRONG GREEN TEA
1½ OUNCES VANILLA VODKA
¾ OUNCE SIMPLE SYRUP (SEE PAGE 7)
¾ OUNCE LIGHT CREAM (OR VANILLA SOY MILK), OPTIONAL
MINT LEAF, FOR GARNISH

Combine the green tea, vanilla vodka, simple syrup, and light cream in a cocktail shaker filled with ice and shake vigorously. Strain into a chilled martini glass. Float a mint leaf on top.

Power TINI

2 OUNCES VODKA
SPLASH OF LIME JUICE
4 OUNCES POWER DRINK (E.G., RED BULL)
LIME WHEEL, FOR GARNISH

Combine the vodka and lime juice in a cocktail shaker filled with ice and shake vigorously. Strain into a chilled martini glass. Top off with the power drink. Garnish with a lime wheel.

97

HERBAL MARTINIS

The following martinis all contain various herbal supplements, reputed to enhance the libido and increase stamina and energy. However, they should not be consumed as replacements to your current vitamin or herbal regimen. If you are taking any medications or other herbal supplements, please consult your doctor first.

Ginseng SLING

A variation on the classic Singapore Sling, with an added dose of ginseng. Ginseng has been known to increase stamina as well as relieve stress.

- 3 BING CHERRIES, PITTED, PLUS AN EXTRA FOR GARNISH
- 1¼ OUNCES PLYMOUTH GIN
- ¾ OUNCE CHERRY HEERING LIQUEUR
- 2 OUNCES APPLE JUICE
- 1 DROPPER SIBERIAN GINSENG (ELEUTHERO), ABOUT 20 DROPS
- 2 TO 3 DASHES OF ANGOSTURA BITTERS

In a cocktail shaker, mash the pitted cherries together with the gin and cherry liqueur. Add the apple juice, ginseng, and bitters, fill with ice, and shake vigorously. Strain into a chilled martini glass. Garnish with a whole bing cherry.

98

Hocus Focus MARTINI

Ginkgo biloba, used in Chinese medicine, is believed to sharpen memory, improve cognitive function, and increase circulation. Yerba maté is a tea that has been known to have the same effects as caffeine and sugar, without the crash. It combats fatigue and stimulates the mind.

- ¼ CUP OF FRESH CHOPPED PINEAPPLE
- 1½ OUNCES VODKA
- ½ OUNCE TUACA (OR SUBSTITUTE B & B LIQUEUR)
- 1 OUNCE YERBA MATÉ TEA
- 1 DROPPER GINKO BILOBA (ABOUT 20 DROPS)
- 2 OUNCES GINGER BEER
- 2 DRY BAY LEAVES, FOR GARNISH

In a cocktail shaker, mash the pineapple together with the vodka and Tuaca until pulped. Add the yerba maté, ginkgo biloba, and ice. Shake vigorously. Strain into a chilled martini glass. Top off with the ginger beer. Float the dried bay leaves on top.

99

Women's Yin MARTINI

A tempting martini made with damiana, said to enhance sexual potency and relax the mind and body, and *maca,* reputed to increase sexual vitality.

2 OUNCES PAPAYA NECTAR
1 ¼ OUNCES 100% BLUE AGAVE REPOSADO TEQUILA
¾ OUNCE DAMIANA LIQUEUR
½ OUNCE LEMON JUICE
½ OUNCE SIMPLE SYRUP (SEE PAGE 7)
1 DROPPER MACA (ABOUT 20 DROPS)
MINT LEAF, FOR GARNISH

Combine the papaya nectar, tequila, Damiana liqueur, lemon juice, simple syrup, and *maca* in a cocktail shaker filled with ice and shake vigorously. Strain into a martini glass. Garnish with a mint leaf.

100

Men's Yang MARTINI

An alluring martini that naturally enhances the male libido. Made with yerba maté, a natural energizer; *maca,* an aphrodisiac; and apples, the first temptation of man.

101

- 2 BING CHERRIES, PITTED
- 1 APRICOT HALF
- 1 OUNCE GRAND MARNIER
- 1 OUNCE BLENDED SCOTCH
- 1 OUNCE APPLE JUICE
- 1 OUNCE FRESHLY SQUEEZED ORANGE JUICE
- 1 OUNCE YERBA MATÉ TEA
- 1 DROPPER MACA
- RED APPLE SLICE, FOR GARNISH

In a cocktail shaker, mash the cherries and apricot together with the Grand Marnier and scotch until pulped. Add the apple juice, orange juice, yerba maté, *maca,* and ice and shake vigorously. Strain into a chilled martini glass. Garnish with a red apple slice.